SOUTHEND PAST

A photographic record of Southend-on-Sea,
1865-1940

by
J. R. SMITH

Southend Branch Archivist
Essex Record Office

Published by
Essex County Council, Chelmsford
Essex Record Office Publications, No. 73
1979

ISBN 0 900360 52 6

FOREWORD

During the first five years of its existence, the Southend Branch of the Essex Record Office has accumulated an impressively rich collection of more than 5,000 archive photographs of Southend, dating from about 1865, many of them formerly acquired or deposited in the Borough Library, others generously donated to the Record Office over recent years. Together they form a comprehensive pictorial history of the physical development of the town, embracing such subjects as esplanades, housing, piers, roads, schools and tramways. Many of these have been reproduced and exhibited in recent years, and this booklet appears in response to numerous requests that a selection of the best be made available in published form.

Thirty photographs are reproduced, all of which relate to the geographical area of the former County Borough of Southend-on-Sea, now the District Council area. They have been selected for their intrinsic interest; some depict landscapes or townscapes that have altered, sometimes almost beyond recognition, while others show individual buildings that have been demolished. Many of those buildings antedated the growth of Southend and its environs in the nineteenth and twentieth centuries, and belonged to an earlier rural society and environment, nearly all traces of which have disappeared.

Within its admittedly limited scope, this booklet can do no more than whet the appetite of its readers. Many other photographs in the Record Office's collections merit publication and whole aspects of Southend's history remain unmentioned. Indeed, the town still awaits a detailed history which would trace its physical and institutional development from a minor Georgian watering-place to its present-day function as a major residential town and busy administrative centre. The work of the Southend Branch Record Office and the generosity of those who have deposited records with us will, it is hoped, one day make that history possible.

Thanks are due to Mr N. Hammond, Senior Photographer, Essex Record Office, and Mr J. Wood, Photographer, Southend General Hospital, for skilled assistance with the illustrations. I am also grateful for the valuable criticism and suggestions of the County Archivist, Mr V. W. Gray, and of my staff at Southend, Jennifer Butler and Jane Sprenger.

J. R. Smith
Essex Record Office
Southend Branch
November 1979

Ingram's Warm Baths, Southend, *c.* 1865

The Baths were built in 1804 by a Mr Ingram and were one of Southend's chief attractions as a resort for the gentry and nobility. In 1824 they were described as consisting of "a neat cottage, exceedingly well fitted up with warm baths, which are constantly supplied by means of machinery . . .". By 1841 they were owned by Thomas Ingram, shown here with his family. The Baths were on a site below the Royal Hotel, at the eastern end of the Shrubbery. The pony was employed to pump the water from an artesian well. The outline of the Royal Hotel may be seen through the trees.

In 1879 they were demolished to enable the Local Board of Health to construct a new Pier toll-house and approaches.

Southend Lifeboat, November 1879

In 1876 the Royal National Lifeboat Institution stationed a lifeboat, the *Springwell*, at Harwich, and three years later in 1879 sent a small lifeboat to Southend, following representations from the Rev. Frederick Thackeray, vicar of Shopland and cousin of the author William Makepeace Thackeray. He lived at 9 Royal Terrace and his eldest son, Frederick, had been drowned at sea in 1867.

Called the '*Boys of England and Edwin J. Brett*, the boat was self-righting, 24 feet long and designed primarily for rowing. She cost £350, much of which was raised by a fund in the *Boys of England* magazine, whose owner, Edwin Brett, came to Southend on 13 November 1879 to christen the boat which bore his name.

The lifeboat station was on the Pier Head from which the boat was launched by davits. During 10 years' service at Southend (1879-1889) the *Boys of England and Edwin J. Brett* saved a total of 23 lives. The photograph shows her, with the crew, beached at Southend; in the background is the original wooden pier, built in 1829-30.

Royal Library, *c.* 1890

Rennison and Tarry's Library was built in the 1790s at the top of Pier Hill, opposite the Royal Hotel. It became known as the Royal Library following the three-month stay at Southend of Princess Caroline of Wales (wife of George, Prince of Wales, later George IV) and her daughter, Princess Charlotte, in 1804. The gentleman author of *A Guide to Southend* (1824) noted that: "It has a good reading room, and is well supplied with London and provincial papers, periodical publications, etc. This is the only library in the town, and is well attended, particularly in the evenings, when there are raffles and other amusements of the same kind". It was still popular half a century later when the proprietor described it as containing "from two to three thousand volumes, consisting of the most popular works and leading periodicals of the day. . . . It is open to both ladies and gentlemen and a moderate subscription by the week, month, or year comprehends both Library and Reading Room."

All except the back and side walls were demolished in June 1914.

Pier Hill Buildings, Southend, 1898

In 1893 Southend Corporation Pier Committee sponsored a competition for the development of the sloping site between the Pier Toll House and the Shrubbery. Of the fourteen designs submitted, that of the Southend architect, James Thompson, was adopted, but it was not until December 1895 that the Corporation decided to proceed with the scheme. Building began in 1896 and on 29 April 1897 the *London Magazine* reported:

> This Pier-hill scheme . . . is now well on the way, and by the time the season is in full swing it will be completed. The Scheme comprises . . . sea water baths . . . shelters, restaurants . . . promenade and arcade. The bathrooms number forty, twenty for gentlemen and twenty for ladies . . . lavatories, cloak-rooms, waiting rooms . . . are provided . . . in first-class style throughout. . . . The first promenade plan provides a very picturesque photographic studio . . . clock tower . . . bandstand of handsome design . . . large reading room and shelter, and several shops. . . . The second level promenade provides additional shops, and also pleasantly situated alcoves with seats. . . . The scheme is calculated to be . . . very profitable . . . and . . . will materially assist in reducing the rates.

Building problems and disputes between the contractor and Corporation delayed the opening, however, until the summer of 1898, and the final cost was £14,675. The photograph was taken in spring 1898, shortly before completion.

The Buildings were demolished by Southend Corporation in 1977, having been empty and neglected for several years.

Chalkwell Beach, *c.* 1904

This photograph of Chalkwell Beach looking towards Leigh was probably taken in the summer of 1904. The bathing machines at the water's edge and the changing tents on the right were a common sight at all English seaside resorts. At Southend their use was compulsory, for the Corporation's byelaws forbade public undressing on the beach by adults, and offenders were liable to a fine of 20 shillings.

In the nineteenth century the popularity of a resort could be measured by the number and quality of its bathing machines; women took to wearing voluminous bathing costumes but men continued to bathe naked, and the machines served "to protect modesty against . . . inquisitive eyes". Having changed inside the machine the bather, still concealed from public view, descended into the water from the rear. At Southend the machines were hauled out of the sea by winches.

By the beginning of the twentieth century bathing tents or cabins on the beach began to replace the cumbersome bathing machines (although the latter could still be seen at Southend in the 1920s) and bathing costumes had become universal for both sexes.

Westcliff Esplanade, Summer 1905

During the years 1903-6 Southend Corporation constructed sea walls and promenades at Chalkwell and Westcliff Espalanades. Chalkwell Esplanade, a strip of land between the Chalkwell Hall Estate and the sea stretching from Chalkwell Station in the west to Crowstone Avenue in the east, was granted to the Corporation by the Chalkwell Hall Syndicate in March 1903. The Corporation agreed to construct and maintain a sea wall, public road and esplanade and the Syndicate contributed £8,000 towards the cost of the works. Westcliff Esplanade ran from Crowstone Avenue in the west to Shorefield Gardens in the east. Facing stone for the walls was shipped from Kent in sailing barges, while much of the infill material was supplied by contractors digging underground railway tunnels in London.

The photograph shows the eastern end of Westcliff Esplanade near Shorefield Gardens, which was completed and opened in 1905. Improvement of Western Esplanade, from this point to the Pier, began in 1910.

The Palmeira Towers Hotel, on the left of the photograph, was demolished in 1978.

Halfway House, Southchurch, *c.* 1906

The 'Halfway House' public house was built on Southchurch Beach (now called Eastern Esplanade) about 1870, when it stood with a group of humble cottages in an isolated position. Ribbon development along the seafront stretched east from Southend only as far as the gas works, and the public house took its name from its situation approximately halfway between Old Southend and Shoeburyness. To the north lay Wyatts Farm and to the east extensive brickfields. In 1882, when Abraham Robinson was licensee, it was known as 'The Halfway Tavern'.

When this photograph was taken about 1906 the road was unmade and there was no sea wall, but the scene was soon to change. By 1909 the road had been widened, a sea wall constructed, and Corporation tramway extension to 'Halfway House' opened in November. The tavern was completely rebuilt shortly after the First World War, and renamed the 'Halfway House Hotel'.

Pier Head Extension, 12 September 1908

The first pier, 1,500 feet in length, was opened in 1830, and was extended to a total length of one and a quarter miles in 1846. It was acquired by the Local Board in 1875 and replaced by the present structure in 1889-91.

The Pier Head Extension was begun in 1896 and opened in 1898. It extended 150 feet south of the former Pier Head, which was becoming difficult for ships to reach at low water because of silting in the Swatch, and was specially adapted for passenger steamboat traffic. In 1907 the Corporation's Pier Committee approved a scheme for the construction of an upper promenade deck on the Extension. The contractors were Messrs C. Wall and Co. of Grays. The formal opening of the promenade deck by the Mayor, Alderman J. C. Ingram, took place on 25 July 1908. The photograph shows part of the new works, including the bandstand and fog-tower.

The Extension was badly damaged, and the promenade deck destroyed, by fire in 1976.

Southend Loading Pier, 26 July 1913

The first loading pier was built adjoining the east side of the passenger pier in 1834. It was constructed of timber and stone, and extended 234 feet from the shore. When the original passenger pier was replaced with the present iron structure in 1889-91 a new loading pier was built opposite the 'Ship' inn, but it soon became inadequate to handle the increasing volume of trade, and in 1910 Southend Corporation resolved to build the present loading pier with up-to-date crane equipment, a short distance to the west of the gas works jetty. In July 1912 the Corporation accepted the lowest tender for the work, that of Mr T. W. Pedrette of Enfield, in the sum of £10,878. The work was completed in 1914.

Most of Southend's maritime trade was carried on by sailing barges. There were about 2,000 of these vessels working on the east coast in 1910, and their flat-bottomed hulls were designed to take the ground at low water. The photograph shows the first barge to use the new loading pier.

Westcliff Swimming Bath, May 1915

In November 1911 Southend Corporation resolved to build a swimming bath at Westcliff in response to applications from the Westcliff Ratepayers' Association and other bodies for bathing facilities at all states of the tide. The bath was to be constructed within one of the large sea wall bastions planned as part of the scheme to widen Western Esplanade in 1912. Following a protracted period of discussion about the design it was agreed in July 1913 to build an unheated, open-air bath measuring 300 feet by 70 feet, with a depth ranging from 2 feet 6 inches at the east end to 6 feet at the west end, and with a deeper diving area. The work of building the bath within the bastion was carried out by Messrs Davey and Armitage of Elmer Avenue, Southend, for £8,473, and was completed in the spring of 1915. The photograph shows the bath in use shortly after the formal opening on 1 May 1915 by the Mayor, Alderman Joseph Francis. Plant for water filtration, heating and purification was installed in 1936.

The bath was closed in October 1969. During the summer of 1970 it was used for displaying trained dolphins, and at the end of that year the Corporation let it for conversion into a private leisure and sports complex.

The Cliffs Bandstand, September 1923

This decorative Edwardian bandstand, popularly known as the 'Cakestand', was erected on the Cliffs at Cliff Town Parade in 1909 by Messrs Walter Macfarlane and Co. of Glasgow at a cost of £750, replacing an earlier wooden bandstand which had been moved from the site to the Happy Valley. The formal opening by the Mayoress, Mrs J. C. Ingram, on 29 May 1909, was followed by a programme of music from the band of the Royal Marines.

The 'Cakestand' became a very popular attraction for summer visitors for many years, particularly as a venue for military bands. It was officially described in 1950 as ''a more than usually ornate and satisfactory example of a typical seaside bandstand of the later Victorian to Edwardian period. Possibly the most interesting example of its kind extant at a seaside resort''. But its 'High Edwardian' styling was out of favour with the corporation when, in 1956, the decision was taken to demolish it and replace it with a more modern type of entertainment platform.

The Public Hall, Alexandra Street, Southend, 1872

The Public Hall was built in 1872 at a cost of about £3,000. It contained a large hall with stage, used for concerts and other entertainments, a club room, and the offices of Southend Local Board, the predecessor of the Borough Council. It also served as a court room for sittings of Rochford Petty Sessions before a Sessions House was built in Alexandra Street in 1883.

By 1893 it was being used as the Alexandra Theatre. In 1894 it was acquired by Mr F. Marlow, and converted into a theatre called the Empire, but was destroyed by fire the following year. On Whit Monday 1896 Mr Marlow's rebuilt and enlarged Empire Theatre, with seating for 1,500 people, was opened on the site. This building stood until 1920 when it was replaced by the Rivoli cinema, renamed the A.B.C. about 1961.

The photograph shows the Public Hall shortly before it was opened in 1872.

Bell Wharf, Leigh, 26 July 1923

At the beginning of the nineteenth century the only centres of population within the present-day town were Prittlewell village, the infant but developing seaside resort of Southend, a mile to the south, and the small port of Leigh, alongside Leigh Creek. Leigh's population in 1801 was only 570, but the arrival of the railway in the 1850s led to its development as a small resort, mostly for yachtsmen, and the opening of the direct line to London in 1888 made it a dormitory town for the capital. Its population rose from 1,370 in 1851 to 3,667 in 1901 and 15,031 in 1921. In 1897 Leigh became an Urban District with a Council of twelve members, and was incorporated in the Borough of Southend in 1913.

Early in the nineteenth century Lawrence Lazarus, coal merchant and distiller, constructed a landing place opposite the 'Bell' public house, with a tramway for carrying coal ashore. It was reconstructed in 1853-54, largely with rubble from the old 'Bell' inn which had been demolished to make way for the railway track, and was thenceforth known as Bell Wharf. A new 'Bell Hotel' was constructed just north of the railway line. In 1897 the wharf was conveyed to Leigh-on-Sea U.D.C. for £185 "subject to such right as now exists for fishermen to land fish and bring them to shore free of toll".

When this photograph was taken Southend Corporation workmen were re-laying the wharf crane rails in readiness for the arrival of a new electric crane which was to replace the old steam crane.

Leigh Hall, Leigh, *c*. 1890

Leigh Hall, ancient seat of the manor of Leigh, stood about 1/4-mile north-east of the parish church, between the present-day Leigh Hall Road and Oakleigh Park Drive, just south of Pall Mall. The photograph shows the south front. The house, according to Philip Benton in 1867, was said to date from 1561 and was originally larger, probably with a western wing.

Following the death in 1863 of Lady Olivia Sparrow, lady of the manor, ownership of the lordship and of Leigh Hall Farm was split. The farm (then 225 acres) was purchased in September 1864 for £8,042 8s. by James Thomas Smith, a Kent coal merchant, who let it in 1879 for 14 years to Arthur and Pendrill Bentall, farmers. Leigh Hall became Pendrill's family home until his death in 1898.

Housing development began in 1891, and in February 1893 Smith sold most of the land together with part of Ellen Elm Farm and both farmhouses to Frederick Ramuz (Mayor of Southend, 1898) for £9,200. The property, then named the Leigh Hall Estate, was described by Ramuz's Land Company as 'The New Eldorado'. During the next decade regular auctions of building plots took place in a marquee on the estate. The Hall was sold to William Taylor, timber merchant, between 1900 and 1905, and demolished about 1907. The site is still occupied by Taylor's timber yard.

Strand Wharf and Cottages, Leigh, 1940

Strand Wharf belonged to the manor of Leigh which levied charges for beaconage and for the landing of goods. The five tenements shown here were originally two separate timber-framed structures. The two tenements at the southern (seaward) end were built about the middle of the nineteenth century, while the three to the north (one a cross-wing and two with dormers) originally formed one large house owned early in the seventeenth century by Richard Chester (d.1632), a master of Trinity House, who may have built it. Certainly it was the home of a man of considerable wealth and some of the rooms were richly panelled in oak.

In 1773 Chester's former house was described as being let to the Overseers of the Poor for the use as the parish workhouse, and it was known locally thereafter as the Alms House. When it was first let for this purpose is not clear, but it was not earlier than 1712 and probably much nearer 1773. By 1790 it was no longer the workhouse and had been divided into three tenements.

In 1939 all five tenements were purchased by Southend Corporation and demolished the following year. The photograph was taken shortly after demolition began.

Leigh House, Leigh, *c*. 1926

Leigh House stood at the extreme south end of what is now known as Elm Road, about 50 yards north-west of the church. It was a timber-framed structure built about 1600, and was originally known as Black House. Its most famous owner was Anthony Deane (?1638-1721), the greatest naval shipbuilder of his time. Although his chief homes were at Portsmouth and Harwich he occasionally resided at Leigh, which was then a minor shipbuilding centre. In 1670 Deane sold Leigh House to Thomas Printupp of Leigh, mariner, for £200. From 1792 to 1815 it was inhabited by John Loten, Collector of Customs for Leigh for 33 years. It then passed to his only and illegitimate son John Loten upon whose death (*ante* 1844) it was sold by his trustees to David Montague of Leigh, who owned Leigh Pottery and Brickworks. The mid-nineteenth century remodelling of the house was almost certainly the work of Montague. From about 1912 to 1927 it was occupied by Dr William Douglas Watson, physician and surgeon.

Leigh House was demolished by Southend Corporation in 1927 when Broadway West was constructed.

Toll House or Turnpike Cottage, London Road, Leigh, 1900

The road from the 'Eagle and Child' inn at Shenfield to Billericay and Rayleigh, with branches to Leigh and Rochford, was turnpiked in 1747. The Leigh branch ran *via* Victoria House corner, then along London Road, terminating at the junction with Eastwood Road. At this point there were toll gates across both London Road (on the east side of the junction) and Eastwood Road, and tolls for admission on to the turnpike road were paid by all users except foot travellers.

Turnpike Cottage was built between 1845 and 1851, probably replacing an earlier building. After about 1840 the growth of railway transport led to a decline in the tolls received and the Turnpike Trusts were abolished in the 1860s. Leigh Turnpike Cottage was then used as a private residence until it was demolished by Southend Corporation in July 1923 during the widening of London Road. Part of the former garden is now occupied by public lavatories in Eastwood Road.

The photograph was taken in the summer of 1900. At that time the owner was Alexander Underwood Higgins of Lapwater Hall, surveyor, property speculator and developer, and the occupiers were the Barwell family. Thirsty travellers could stop here and be refreshed with tea, cider, mineral water, ginger beer, lemonade or soda water.

Eastwood Road and Blenheim Chase, Leigh, 29 August 1922

In 1864 maintenance of roads in Leigh became the responsibility of the newly-formed Rochford Highway Board. When Leigh obtained Urban District status in 1897 responsibility for roads was transferred to that authority, where it remained until the incorporation of Leigh into Southend Borough Council in 1913.

A green lane or chaseway nearly three miles long led through fields from Earls Hall (Prittlewell) in the east, to Eastwood Road in the west, passing close by Brickhouse and Gowles farmhouses. This photograph was taken at the western termination of the chaseway, at Eastwood Road, now the site of a roundabout. The bowler-hatted figure is standing in Eastwood Road, then a pretty country lane leading to London Road, half a mile to the south.

Shortly after the photograph was taken work began on the conversion of part of the ancient chaseway, between Eastwood Road and Winchmore Gardens, into a dual carriageway road.

Corporation Tram Offices, Victoria Circus, Southend, May 1910

The rapid growth of Southend in the last quarter of the nineteenth century led to a demand for an efficient public transport system. In 1896 the Light Railways Act was passed to encourage the construction of tramways, and in September 1899 the Board of Trade authorised Southend Corporation to build a series of routes radiating from Victoria Circus. The service commenced in July 1901, and,despite teething troubles, proved an immediate success.

The service was considerably expanded and improved between 1908 and the outbreak of the Great War, and included the construction of a ticket office and waiting room on an island site at Victoria Circus. Work on the ticket office began towards the end of 1909 and was completed the following May. The striking clock in the turret was a gift from Mr R. A. Jones, a Southend jeweller and local benefactor. It was demolished in 1932 when major road alterations took place at Victoria Circus.

The Theatre de Luxe cinema on the right of the photograph was opened in 1908. It was demolished in 1923-4, and the site was redeveloped as part of J. F. Dixon's department store.

Brightwell Estate Company's Marquee, London Road, Westcliff, 11 August 1908

The Edwardian period saw the biggest and fastest growth of Southend as a dormitory and holiday town. The population of the borough, which then comprised the ancient ecclesiastical parishes of Prittlewell and Southchurch, rose from 27,299 in 1901 to 62,723 in 1911.

Its development as a residential town was chiefly the work of private estate developers and property speculators like Frederick Francis Ramuz of Shorefields, Westcliff, a solicitor and member of the Southend Corporation, whose Land Company of Cheapside, London, was the largest company of the kind operating in south Essex. The Brightwell Estate Company was owned by John Rumbelow Brightwell, better known as a High Street draper. Like Ramuz he was a member of the Corporation, and was Mayor in 1894.

Building plots were sold at auctions or by private treaty in marquees like that in the photograph, set up by the Brightwell Estate Company at the corner of London Road and Brightwell Avenue on the Westcliff Park Estate. The wooden hoarding heralded the building shortly afterwards of the present-day Westcliff branch of Lloyd's Bank.

Woodfield Park Drive, Chalkwell, 25 January 1922

While the private property development companies laid out roads and sold building plots, it was often many years before Southend Corporation was able to supply public utilities such as sewers, paving, street surfacing and lighting. Many inhabitants will remember street scenes like this, with no surface water drains, sewers or paving and a road surface like a farm track in winter.

Woodfield Park Drive forms part of the Chalkwell Park (Building) Estate, developed by the Land Company from 1896. The plots were sold at auctions held at regular intervals in a marquee near the Grand Hotel, Leigh, and a special train was run from Fenchurch Street on auction days, the return fare to Leigh being 2s. 6d. Most of the plots sold for very low prices; for example, in October 1901, Harold John Sharp of Holloway, London, purchased two house plots in Woodfield Park Drive for a total of £50. As a further inducement to purchase, the Land Company offered free conveyances.

East Street, Prittlewell, *c.* 1891

Until the present century Prittlewell was a pretty rural village grouped mainly to the south and west of the parish church. When this photograph was taken it still retained the appearance and some of the functions of a rural market centre. Its three streets, East, West and North Streets, contained many fine medieval and later timber-framed houses some of which are shown in this view of East Street, looking towards the junction with North and West Streets. Before the opening of Victoria Avenue in 1889 the route to Southend was either along East Street, Sutton Road and Old Southend Road, to reach the sea-front at the 'Minerva' public house, or along West Street and North Road to join London Road at the 'Cricketers' inn.

Traders in East Street in 1891 included a wheelwright, baker, cabinetmaker, shoemaker, two blacksmiths, a dairyman, beer retailer, upholsterer, draper and grocer. Also in East Street was the village school (see page 24).

22

North Street, Prittlewell, *c.* 1891

By the turn of the century, the fields and woods of the ancient parish of Prittlewell (an area of nearly 3,500 acres of land, which included Southend, Milton and Westcliff) were rapidly giving way to housing estates. The population had risen from 4,589 in 1871, to 12,272 in 1891. By 1921 the population of the County Borough (which then comprised the three ancient parishes of Leigh, Prittlewell and Southchurch) had reached 106,000, and Prittlewell village was becoming surrounded by a vast new urban environment.

For centuries the parish church and church-yard had been hidden behind the medieval and later buildings in North Street (renamed Victoria Avenue in 1901) and East Street. As early as 1912 Prittlewell Improvement Scheme to enhance the church's surroundings by the demolition of this property was put forward, but it was not until after the war that changes were made. The Prittlewell War Memorial Scheme of 1918 linked the objectives of the original Scheme with the sacrifices of the parishioners during the Great War, and during the next twenty years these old buildings were acquired and demolished by Southend Corporation, which used the opportunity for road widening.

Former Prittlewell Village Schoolhouse, *c.* 1895

By 1634 a timber-framed messuage called Glynds had been built on the east side of North Street, immediately south of Prittlewell Bridge (now the south corner of Priory Crescent and Victoria Avenue). In 1727 the parishioners, headed by the Vicar, the Rev. T. Case, persuaded Daniel Scratton, lord of the manor of Prittlewell, to endow a school. Glynds became the schoolhouse, and free instruction in reading, writing, the catechism and "principles of the Christian religion according to the usage of the Church of England" was given to ten boys of poor Prittlewell parishioners. The endowment was enlarged by Scratton in 1739 to provide instruction for 16 poor boys.

In 1817, in order to accommodate more children and to include girls, a brick extension to the rear was constructed for the exclusive use of boys. The old schoolhouse was thenceforth appropriated to girls. In 1836 it was reported that there were about 80 children in the school. The minimum age for admission was seven years and all children except the 16 boys admitted under the 1739 endowment paid one penny a week.

In March 1868 new larger premises were opened in East Street and the original schoolhouse and extension were sold for £400 the following year. It was demolished shortly after the Second World War.

Roots Hall, Prittlewell, *c.* 1899

Roots Hall stood on the north side of West Street, a short distance from North Street. A timber-framed structure with later alterations, it probably dated from the eighteenth century, but since it stood on a very much older cellar it was doubtless a rebuilding of an earlier house. It was known as Roots Hall by 1716, but this was a corruption of 'Rowards' by which name it was known as early as 1511.

In 1792 it was owned by John Durrival Kemp of Southchurch, miller, and occupied by Thomas Seacole, apothecary. About 1813 it was purchased by Michael Saward of Thorpe Hall, Southchurch, and by 1815 it belonged to Captain Robert Scallon who had married Saward's daughter Rebecca. In 1839 the grounds, which lay chiefly north of the house, amounted to four acres. It was purchased in December 1876 by Daniel Gossett (Mayor of Southend, 1893) who lived there until 1899 in which year the house and garden were offered for sale by auction, most of the grounds having already been sold off. A few months later it was demolished.

Most of the former grounds are now incorporated in the Southend United Football Club Stadium, appropriately named Roots Hall.

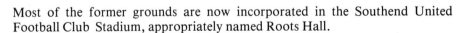

Reynolds, West Street, Prittlewell, *c.* 1890

On the opposite side of West Street, on a site now occupied by the Southend Amateur Boxing Club and the Blue Boar extension, stood Reynolds. It was a timber-framed structure built in the fourteenth century as a single-storied hall-house with two jettied cross-wings, one of which (the eastern) was refaced early in the nineteenth century. The name is probably to be associated with Robert Reynolds who owned and lived in a house in Prittlewell and who was accused of murdering his wife in 1388. In 1841 it belonged to William Weld Wren of Eastwood, farmer, and was occupied by a Mr Livermore.

The figure on the left of this photograph, with bowler hat and mutton-chop whiskers, is William Wallis, village grocer and postmaster for about 30 years from *c.* 1868 to his retirement *c.* 1898.

When Reynolds was demolished in 1906 the magnificent mid-fifteenth-century fireplace and chimney at the east end of the hall was taken to the Victoria and Albert Museum where it lay in store until it was removed to Southend Museum, Victoria Avenue, early in 1975.

Workhouse Cottages, Sutton Road, Prittlewell, *c.* 1910

Prittlewell Workhouse was built in 1785 by the Overseers of the Poor on the west side of Sutton Road, just north of the junction with East Street. When the Rochford Union Workhouse was built at Rochford in 1837-8 Prittlewell Workhouse was sold to Daniel Scratton of Prittlewell Priory and divided into six tenements. By the opening years of the present century they were known as Mill Hill Cottages. The small, square, brick building with the pyramidal tiled roof to the right of the main building was the parish "lock-up".

Workhouse inmates were clothed in coarse cloth of a "mixed dark grey colour" and the collar of each coat was marked with a large "P". They were employed mainly in spinning and carding wool. In 1813 the master was allowed 3s. a week for the maintenance of each inmate pauper.

The Workhouse and "lock-up" were demolished by Southend Corporation in 1960.

Prittlewell Pest House, 13 February 1914

Pest houses were an early form of isolation hospital. They were always situated well away from the main centre of population, and inhabitants with highly contagious diseases, notably small-pox, were sent there to prevent the spread of infection.

Prittlewell pest house stood on the east side of Eastwood Lane, just south of Prittle Brook, where Cavendish Gardens now joins Kingsway. It was a timber-framed building, erected in the eighteenth century. By 1840 it was no longer a pest house, and had been converted into two tenements occupied by John Wallace and Mrs Wakeling.

In 1913 it was purchased from a Mr Oakham of Laindon by Southend Corporation for £350, and demolished in February 1914 in order to widen Eastwood Lane. The photograph shows it in the early stages of demolition.

Bournes Green Farmhouse, Southchurch, *c.* 1914

Bournes Green Farmhouse, otherwise known as Daines Farm, stood on the west side of Thorpe Lane (no longer in existence at this point) near the junction with Shoebury Road. It was a timber-framed structure built about 1400 and was an excellent example of a medieval house with a single-storied hall and two jettied cross-wings. A first floor was inserted in the hall about 1600 and dormer windows were let into the roof. The central chimney was built about the same time. It was occupied by John Daines, farmer, in the middle years of the nineteenth century, and in the last quarter of the century it became the home of the Dunnett family, including F. S. Dunnett (born *c.* 1856) who was employed as a lad by John Daines and who subsequently served as a member of Southend Corporation.

The house was demolished in 1959 in order to redevelop the site, which is now occupied by modern houses.

Cockethurst, Eastwood, *c.* 1925

The red-brick Cockethurst stands at the junction of Snakes Lane and Whitehouse Road. It has a complicated building history, and the earliest work is of the sixteenth century. By the late sixteenth or early seventeenth century it had come into the possession of the Vassall family; Samuel Vassall, eldest son of John Vassall, alderman and merchant of London, lived here and was probably responsible for major alterations and rebuilding about 1640.

Although their home in the eighteenth century was Eastwoodbury, the Vassalls retained Cockethurst until the death, in 1808, of Asser Vassall, singled out for comment by the agricultural writer Arthur Young for his dislike of "new-fangled whims" in farming.

The house now passed into the hands of his son-in-law William Weld Wren, husband of his only daughter and heir, Mary. William Weld made Cockethurst his home and carried out extensive alterations; he was still living there in 1842 when there were 146 acres of land and several cottages belonging to Cockethurst Farm. Philip Benton described the land in 1867 as being "very fertile", in recent years it has all been built over with modern houses.